EAY-797

Best wishes to a good sport,

Richard Armour

❧ ALL IN SPORT ❧

♛ BOOKS BY RICHARD ARMOUR

BIOGRAPHY AND LITERARY CRITICISM
Barry Cornwall: A Biography of Bryan Waller Procter
The Literary Recollections of Barry Cornwall
Coleridge the Talker (with Raymond F. Howes)

PLAY
To These Dark Steps (with Bown Adams)

LIGHT VERSE
All in Sport
An Armoury of Light Verse
For Partly Proud Parents
Golf Bawls
Leading with My Left
Light Armour
The Medical Muse
Nights with Armour
Privates' Lives
Punctured Poems
Yours for the Asking

PROSE HUMOR AND SATIRE
American Lit Relit
Armour's Almanac
The Classics Reclassified
A Diabolical Dictionary of Education
Drug Store Days

All in Sport

⚑ BY RICHARD ARMOUR ⚑

WITH DRAWINGS BY LEO HERSHFIELD

⚑

MC GRAW-HILL BOOK COMPANY

New York   Toronto   St. Louis   Düsseldorf

Mexico   Panama

FIRST EDITION

Library of Congress Cataloging in Publication Data

Armour, Richard Willard, date
  All in Sport

  Poems.
  I. Title.
  PS3501.R55A78   811'5'2   72-2672
  ISBN 0-07-002302-6

♈ ACKNOWLEDGMENTS

The following verses were published initially in *Sports Illustrated* and are reprinted by permission:

> End of a Televised Fight; Tell Me About It; Lame Excuse; Dig Those Crazy Bounces; Italian Style; Serving Them Right; Journey's End; Last Blast; Hockey or Hackey?; Good Looking; Distinction; Mistaken Identity; Who's Lacrosse, Dad?; Stringing Along; On the Up and Up; Canny Mountaineer; Unkindest Cut; Can You Tie This?; Plane and Fancy; Ternabout; Present Accounted For; Bullet Proof; His Timing Is Off; Good Skate; Listen to This.

Copyright © 1955, 1956, 1957, 1958, 1959, 1960 by Time Inc.

A few verses are taken from my *Golf Is a Four-Letter Word*, Copyright © 1962.

✠ FOREWORD

The word sport is an abbreviation of disport, which comes from the Old French *desporter*, to carry away. When you are involved with a sport you disport yourself and are carried away from work or your wife (or husband) or whatever you are trying to escape. Sport, therefore, is that which diverts and entertains, a pastime or amusement.

But the word is more complicated than that. In biology, a sport is a sudden spontaneous deviation or variation from type, a mutation. And in ordinary usage, sport has meanings as various as a theatrical performance, a plaything, a pleasantry, a subject of derision, a gambler, a bon vivant, and (unfortunately obsolete) dalliance, wantonness, amorous play. The verb to sport can mean to make merry, to wager, to waste in gaming or riotous living, to wear something in public ostentatiously, to spend lavishly, to utter in an easy or sportive manner, to treat to food or drink, to force something open, to frolic, or to exhibit bud variation.

I myself took another tack when trying to define the word. I wrote the following, entitled "A Short Definition of Sport":

> Exercise
> In disguise.

This is an aspect of sport overlooked by the lexicographers, most of them, like Samuel Johnson, sedentary men. My definition is distinctive in that it is shorter than any of the dictionary definitions. Also, unlike anything thought up by Webster, it rhymes.

That is about all I can say also for the verses in this little book: they are short and they rhyme. They scan, too, if you read them right. There is no use analyzing them for symbolism or hidden meaning or for the influence of Milton, John Donne, or T. S. Eliot. Assistant professors who wish to publish and thereby be promoted to associate professor are advised to look elsewhere, much as I should like a scholarly review of the book in one of the learned journals.

Despite the definition of sport, above, as "dalliance, wantonness, amorous play," the verses in this book are singularly without prurience. Golf, when you come to think of it (as I have done), is full of phallic symbols. So, for that matter, is bowling. I could have written something unprintable (if anything is, these days) about the pole vault, and I am beginning to see the possibilities for a best seller, made into an X-rated movie, about horseshoes.

But, though I have knowingly forfeited bestsellerdom and a fling in Hollywood, I have kept this book clean. I hope no one will be offended by my reference to loving cups. I suggested to Leo Hershfield that in his drawing he put clothes on them, but he pointed out that this is on the last page of the book, and few readers will get that far.

R.A.

❦ ALL IN SPORT ❦

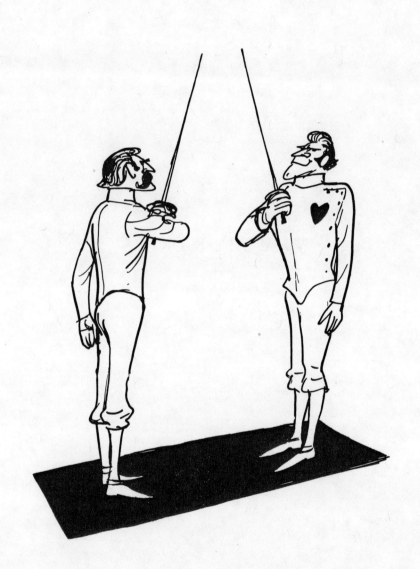

⚜ GOOD SPORTSMANSHIP

Good sportsmanship we hail, we sing.
It's always pleasant when you spot it.
There's only one unhappy thing:
You have to lose to prove you've got it.

⚑ MAXIMUM SECURITY

He's the star indeed of the prison team
And quite a phenomenon.
The reason is that he is a pro,
While everyone else is a con.

⚏ BOUNDER

This basketballer's very quick.
He plays upon a pogo stick.
No one can match the lad at rebounds,
For every time the ball bounds, *he* bounds.

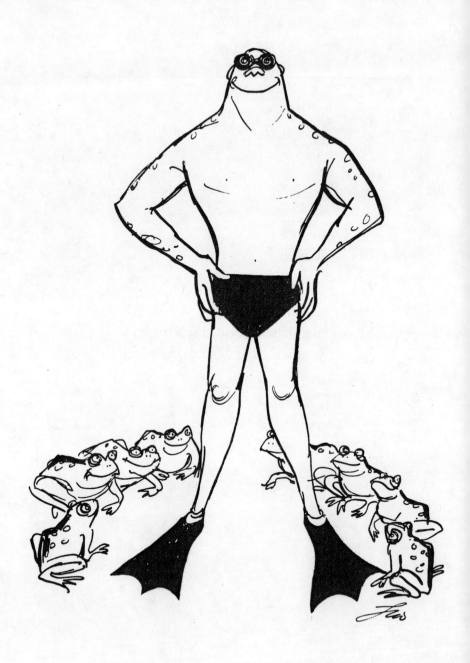

⚔ GETTING A KICK OUT OF IT

Here's a swimmer whose frog kick's the best in
    the world.
It's considered the model, the norm.
In fact it's so good that frogs follow behind
And thoughtfully study his form.

FIGURE IT OUT

This beginner has found that the best device
For making a figure 8
Is not the blades of his skates on ice
But a piece of chalk on a slate.

⚑ ATTENTION BLEACHERITES

Well, here's a home-run slugger
Who's confident, at that.
He autographs the baseball
Before he comes to bat.

⁜ DRIVE WAYS

This golfer drives from tee to green.
He drives with strength and art.
That isn't how he drives the ball,
It's how he drives his cart.

⚑ YOU CAN BET ON IT

There's too much weight on that poor horse,
That's why he sags and slows.
It's not the jockey—no, it's all
That money on his nose.

☗ JOURNEY'S END

The yachtsman's tender where he sits,
The pain is great, one sees.
All day he bravely held his stern
Against a spanking breeze.

♞♜ CHECKED

The cars are lined up, all ready to drag,
But the race is delayed, doggonit.
For the starter has gone with the checkered flag
And he's playing checkers upon it.

THROWN FOR A LOSS

Look sharply, and you'll observe
The oddest occurrence of all:
The pitcher has thrown a curve
But neglected to throw the ball.

☙ LAST BLAST

When all the birds are shot, and still
The urge within him lurks,
He throws his watch into the air—
And then he shoots the works.

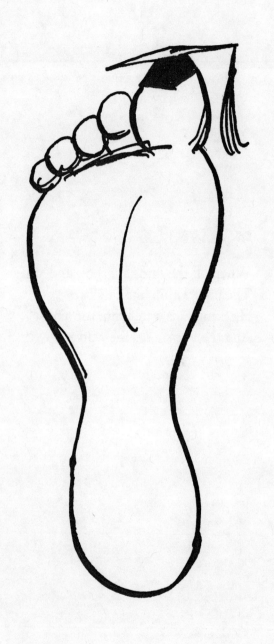

JUST FOR KICKS

This punter has, we understand,
An educated toe.
His education started, and
It stopped, a little low.

ON THE FLY

No fielder gives the fans such fun,
On him you'll find all eyes.
Just watch him leap and reach and run—
He's busy catching flies.

✇ CLEAR SHOT

Is his ball in the rough, right in back of a tree?
No stopping a golfer determined as he.
He carries a saw, and he's strong and he's limber.
Before he shouts "Fore!" you will hear him cry
    "Timber!"

☫ GAY BLADE

He sharpens his skates with affectionate zeal,
The keenest of blades he is craving.
They're not only nice
When he's skating on ice
But equally handy when shaving.

▓ BULLET PROOF

While hunters clad in red get shot,
Here is a hunter who does not.
He saves himself, year after year,
By masquerading as a deer.

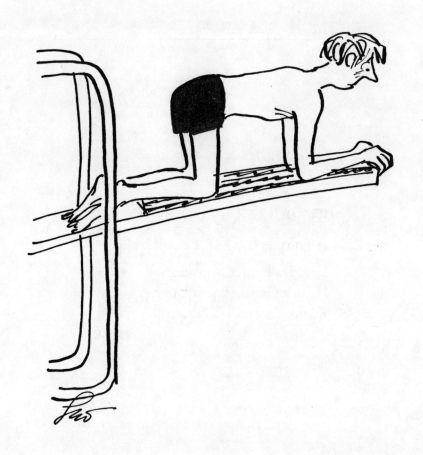

ꖅ HIGH AND DRY

He is no flagpole sitter,
No headline-seeking clown.
He's on the high-dive platform
And scared to climb back down.

ᛟ READY, AIM

After breaking ten rackets,
So great was his verve,
He now uses a cannon
For his cannonball serve.

NEW TWIST

This bowler wears imported tweeds,
A mustache stiff and tinglish,
And monocle. They're what he needs
To give him body English.

☸ BULLY FOR HIM

Why does this brave torero flee?
Should he not fight instead?
He turned his back to bow, and he
Was wearing pants of red.

ꝏ SOLID CITIZEN

He's not very smart,
Or clever, is Ned,
But soccer's one game
Where he uses his head.

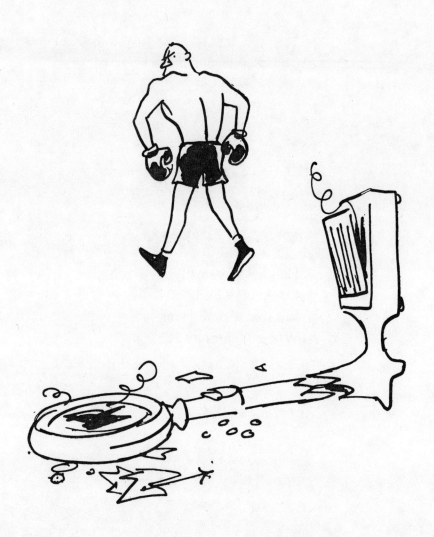

♞ CHEATED

The weighing-in was not so hot.
The boxer took it hard.
He dropped his penny in the slot
But got no fortune card.

GETTING A LIFT

This skier never breaks a bone,
He has no need to frown.
He rides the ski lift up, and then
He rides it right back down.

❖ HANKY PANKY

The handkerchief is dropped—a thrill
Goes through both friends and foes.
The play is stopped, but just until
The ref can blow his nose.

KEEP OFF
THE
EDELWEISS

⚏ CANNY MOUNTAINEER

He knows the mountain passes, so
Climbs not, nor leaps crevasses,
But sits and waits and will not go
Until the mountain passes.

⚜ OFFENSIVE DEFENSIVE

Our team, though quite tall,
Simply can't score at all,
An almost impossible task, it.
What makes it so hard
Is their five-foot-five guard
Who sits up on top of the basket.

⚏ HIS TIMING IS OFF

He has a Sunday punch, you know,
That's powerful and tidy.
He never gets to use it, though,
Because he fights on Friday.

⚏ OUTSIDE CHANCE

No ticket has this football fan,
But he has hope and class.
He waits outside and, running wide,
He hopes to catch a pass.

⚏ HOME FROM THE RANGE

He's practiced so much on the driving range
That now, when a golf game calls,
He's the one in the foursome who looks a bit strange
As he carries a bucket of balls.

⚏ SERVING THEM RIGHT

At Ping-Pong this lad'll
Be heard from some more.
Instead of a paddle
He uses an oar.

ꙮ RIGHT AND RUNG

He carries a ladder
Throughout the last set,
For he thinks he will win
And he can't leap the net.

⚑ EITHER OAR

This oarsman to quicken
His stroke does these chores.
He's picking a chicken
To feather his oars.

⚏ PUT OUT

He put the shot with mighty heave,
Had all his strength behind it.
Where did he put it though? I grieve
To say, no one can find it.

ꙮ GOOD SKATE

Why does this skater never spill?
He's clever, one admits:
He wears his skates not where he stands
But, wisely, where he sits.

✠ CAN YOU TIE THIS?

This fisherman ties
Quite remarkable flies.
They're so lifelike that, to his dismay,
As soon as he's done,
They rise up, one by one,
And gracefully flutter away.

⚡ SAFARI NOT SO GOOD

Pity the hunter, unfortunate one,
Who forgets his bullets or even his gun.
But pity still more one who bags a dandy
But hasn't, alas, a camera handy.

♟ HOCKEY OR HACKEY?

Ice hockey's a game where they give you a stick
And a pad for protecting your shin,
A game where each team beats the other, although
Of course only one can win.

✠ SOUND PRINCIPLE

This maker of tennis equipment is taking
His time; he's a man of great poise.
In a workshop that's padded with cotton he's making
A racket without any noise.

☗ TRAPPED

A sand trap isn't
A sand trap at all.
It doesn't trap sand—
No, it traps the ball.

▓ TAKING THE WRAP

The skier wrapped a scarf around
His neck, snug as can be,
Then, zooming down the slope, he wrapped
Himself around a tree

✠ UNWINDING

This discus thrower's dizzy, though
He's very good at hurling.
The discus landed long ago—
He hasn't yet stopped twirling.

▜ NUMBERS GAME

One runner's safe, one runner's out,
Or so the ump has beckoned.
The one who's safe touched second first,
The one who's out, first second.

❦ LAME EXCUSE

He favors his father,
Some say, but I see,
Since his toe caught that hurdle,
He favors his knee.

♉ PLANE AND FANCY

This pilot skims tree and rooftops,
And terrified people lie flat.
He's licensed for flying solo,
But surely not solo as that.

ꕔ DIG THOSE CRAZY BOUNCES

Our local ball park's
A little tough.
It's sort of a diamond
In the rough.

✵ TOUGH SLEDDING

Hooray! Here the bobsledders come!
Although this cannot be verified,
They're not only thrilled
But terribly chilled
And also terribly terrified.

ꗞ UP FOR GRABS

He grabs a fish
With a fiendish cackle,
Hits it low and hard
With his fishing tackle.

⬚ FUNNY BONE

He has a tennis elbow
That doesn't hurt at all.
There's just the ugly bulge of
That built-in tennis ball.

❦ LISTEN TO THIS

The locker room's one
Place, at least, where a guy,
When the round is done,
Can improve his lie.

⚎ KNOCK ON WOOD

The indoor meets are run on boards
Throughout the months of winter.
That way the runners pick up speed
And now and then a splinter.

☷ POINT BLANK

This pointer knows where the bird is,
But he sits there, relaxed in each joint.
Indifferent? No, what he's heard is
That it isn't polite to point.

🔡 DISTINCTION

Who are these two posed together,
Both looking so pleased and so posh?
The one at the right's a squash champion,
The other's a champion squash.

♯ STRINGING ALONG

This archer has plenty of strings to his bow.
No wonder he's happily humming.
One string is sufficient for shooting, we know
But the others are helpful for strumming.

♛ LIFTING HIS SPIRITS

Those bar bells that he lifts, he tells
Us, have the latest wrinkle.
The bar serves cooling drinks, the bells
Give off a pleasing tinkle.

⚜ REAR VIEW

Here's a horse that, perversely, runs backward,
Yet ever so speedily goes.
It may win by the closest of margins,
But never, of course, by a nose.

♯♯ DIRTY POOL

This player of pocket billiards
Other players completely appalls.
The game, you see, only lasts
Till he's pocketed all of the balls.

⚑ OVER HILL AND DALE

Cross-country running's not for me,
Not in a month of Sundays,
Though I'd run too, I guess, if I
Were caught outdoors in undies.

⚎ HORSEPLAY

This horseshoe pitcher's
Strength's unmatched.
He throws the shoes
With horse attached.

⚑ ON THE UP AND UP

He does a hundred push-ups, though
He's thin and old and gray.
He doesn't do them in a row,
He does them one a day.

✠ LAST LEGS

Here's why the boxer
So happily chuckled:
His legs now are buttoned
That formerly buckled.

⚑ NO HANDICAP

The golfer with the fussy twitch
Went on to win his match.
It wasn't that he had an itch,
He merely played at scratch.

☷ AT HIS PEAK

This mountain climber, broad of hip,
Is one who never fails.
While others try to scale the tip,
He merely tips the scales.

❦ ITALIAN STYLE

I've read of duck-hunting in Venice,
A place where the duck hunter finds,
While awaiting his quarry's arrival,
A use for Venetian blinds.

◊ SCOT FREE

This Scotsman, though he isn't tall,
Plays super scoring basketball.
He takes opponents' kicks and blows
With greatest joy—he loves free throws

♟ HE WINS HANDS DOWN

A handball player is he
Whom opponents can't understand.
He insists on playing, you see,
With a handball shaped like a hand.

ꙮ MISTAKEN IDENTITY

Out from these wrestlers, all entwined,
There comes an anguished groan.
One chap has grabbed and bent a leg
Which is, alas, his own.

⚑ A CATCH TO IT

What tickles this fisherman
Clear to the roots?
There's no fish in his creel,
But there's one in his boots.

▜ GOOD TURN

Just notice this lad
On a turn in the track.
He sticks out his hand
To warn those in back.

CROP CONTROL

This pitcher holds a pitchfork
To help his pitching arm.
Does he pitch hay? No, baseballs.
He's on a baseball farm.

⚏ GOOD LOOKING

It's not her figure skating that
Men find exhilarating.
No, what they're always looking at
Is just her figure, skating.

⚎ UNSTRUNG

His smash was severe,
And wicked his cut,
Yet he didn't laugh
When he split a gut.

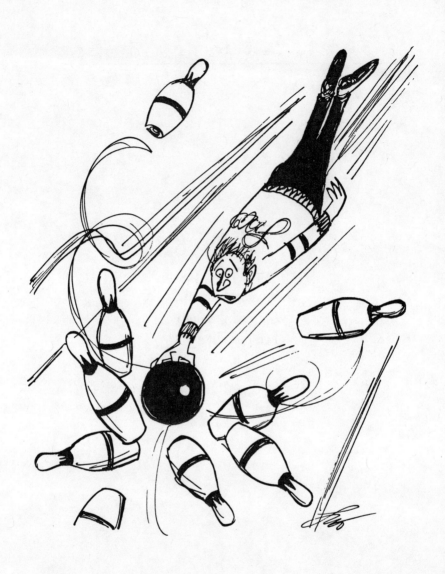

♨ RIGHT DOWN HIS ALLEY

This bowler's bound to make a strike,
His follow-through is great.
Just watch that form. . . . "My thumb is stuck!"
He cries, a bit too late.

✠ ALL A BOARD

A young body surfer we know is so long
And so lean and so flat and so terribly strong
That for making ends meet and to help his career
He hires himself out as a surfboard, we hear.

⬚ PIECE BY PIECE

This golfer's lawn is scrawny,
It's newly seeded loam.
So when he takes a divot,
He really takes it—home.

ᵂᴾ GUNNY SACKS?

He's off for darkest Africa
To win a hunter's fame.
Instead of guns, he's loaded sacks
Upon his native bearers' backs—
He hopes to bag some game.

⚏ ALL WET

This water-polo player
The other players dread.
Because of water in his eyes
He thinks it is the ball and tries
To throw some fellow's head.

♨ UNKINDEST CUT

This golfer has a wicked slice
And quite a follow-through.
That's why his partner, who stood close,
Is on the green in two.

⊕ TELL ME ABOUT IT

Did they block that kick?
What did they do?
The guy in front of me
Blocked my view.

♯ HAMMER AWAY

A ball with chain attached is what
Most hammer throwers hail.
Not he. He throws a hammer and
He hopes to hit a nail.

▓ WHO'S AFRAID?

The scuba diver in his gear
The monstrous fish you'd think would fear.
But no, he looks so very weird
That it's the monstrous fish who're skeered.

AIR-CONDITIONED

To get in a breeze on a hot, stifling day,
Here's a splendid and practically foolproof way:
Just go to the ball park as quick as you can
And sit right in front of a baseball fan.

✠ LIVE BAIT

These fishermen aren't by the stream,
They're huddled in their car.
The fish aren't biting, it would seem,
But the mosquitoes are.

❦ TERNABOUT

This little tern
Now has a brother,
For one good tern
Deserves another.

☠ CAMPUS HERO

He's a four-letter man
At college, we hear.
That's the number of times
He writes home each year.

☠ TAKING PRECAUTIONS

This pole vaulter thinks he will vault so high,
Intent as he is on his task,
That he fixes his gaze on the upper sky
And adjusts his oxygen mask.

☗ MOUNTING SUSPICION

The distinction, of course,
You may note, if you wish,
Between mounting a horse
And mounting a fish.

♯ FOILED

Now here is a fencer who never is touched.
Opponents try hard but can't win.
The fencer, you see, like the fencer he is,
Uses fencing to fence himself in.

✠ WEIGHT RIGHT HERE

They lifted the weight
The weight lifter, of late,
Let fall on his head. They were kind.
And what did he say
When they lugged it away?
He said, "That's a weight off my mind."

⚑ STERLING SERVICE

This courteous chap always loses
At tennis, and here's what's the matter:
Instead of a racket he uses,
When serving, a large silver platter.

▓ END OF A TELEVISED FIGHT

For ten hard rounds they slugged and punched,
With mayhem as their mission.
And all the while he drank and munched,
And he's in worse condition.

✠ UNSOUND CONDITION

They're checking the Ping-Pong ball,
For something, it seems, is wrong.
It pongs when it ought to ping
And it pings when it ought to pong.

❈ SETTLING A SCORE

Two tournament pros, being tied,
Have come to the final payoff.
They've sharpened their clubs into swords
And are in a sudden-death playoff.

☫ COUNT THEM OUT

We're hearing a lot about women's rights,
How men they have hopes of outfoxing.
But until they yell
Of their lefts as well,
They won't be much good at boxing.

ꝃ SKI LIFT

Was the water skier left in the lurch
When the speedboat developed a knock?
No, the water skier, momentum still up,
Towed the speedboat back to the dock.

⚑ WHO'S LACROSSE, DAD?

He's weak on the toss
But good at the get,
For he plays lacrosse
With a butterfly net.

PRESENT ACCOUNTED FOR

At the end of a losing season
They presented the coach with a car,
In which, and they had good reason,
They said that they hoped he'd go far.

ꑭ BAD ACTOR

Here's why I distrust
A wrestler's grimaces:
Where he's hit, where he points
Are two different places.

▀▄ MADE FOR EACH OTHER

Two trophies in the trophy case
Lock handles in a long embrace.
You ask how come, how can this be?
Why not? They're loving cups, you see.